Legends Lives and Loves Along the Inside Passage

By Dudley (CHRIS) Christian

A

Pause For Poetry©

Publication

Acknowledgement:

Special thanks to my wife, Marilyn Christian for compiling, organizing and finalizing the books of my collections. Her photographing and editing skills were vital to all of my works.

ISBN: 978-0-9877501-4-3

First Edition September 2012
Revised Edition June 2017

Copyright © 1971 by Dudley (Chris) Christian
ALL RIGHTS RESERVED.

Any unauthorized reprint or use of this publication is prohibited. No part of this book may be reproduced or transmitted in any form or by any means, electronic or mechanical, including photocopying, recording, or by any information storage and retrieval system without prior written permission from the author.

Cover: Lions Bay view from Highway 99, Vancouver, BC © Marilyn Christian

An Opening Word by the Author...

Many people often ask:

"How do you write and do you have to often rewrite your material?"

I have long summed up my answer to the above with the following:

"A Word, the written word, small purveyor of a thought, so like a thought, once thought, cannot be recalled, so too, a word once writ, should need NOT be re-written, for with such licence, we would but change ... the very substance of the thought."

... DNC © 1970

Dudley (Chris) Christian founded and hosted the first and only "PAUSE FOR POETRY" show dedicated solely to the introduction of new and unknown poets and their works. This TV series ran from 1974 to 1985.

Table of Contents

The Seaman's Reprieve 1
The "Beaulani" Life Plan 2
If We Would Live In Fellowship * 4
Hold On Jeanette Hold On 5
"The Cabaret Comes To Life" 6
If You Be Wrong Admit It * 9
ISABEL ALICE CHRISTIAN WASHINGTON 10
Borning Of A Day 11
Legend Of The Lost Of The "White King" Cruise Ship 12
Solid Water... Solid Water 19
EARTHCHILD... Behind Your Eyes 20
When You Were Born * 22
The Ghostlike Moon 23
Legend Of The Ferry Worker's Ghost 24
The Mortal Man's Approach 30
Man's Ignorance And Inhumanity To Men 33
Skygazing 36
The Shrew Of The Inside Passage 38
Friend ... Aye He Is One 40
The Morning's Softness 43
Youth... With Your Eyes You Flatter Me 44
Dip... Dip... Dip And Dive 48
The Artist Nature 50

Tho Long I May Woo You *	51
Granville Channel	52
The Northwind...	54
Persona Mea...	56
My Part Of My Life *	57
"The Fool Felt Duty Bound"	58
Let Not Thy Authority *	62
Mood Poem Of Thought... (For Grace)	63
"Legend Of The Treasure Ship Below The Pines"	64
Lo, How The High And Mighty *	73
Legend Of The Epitome Of Freedom	74
"Indian ... I Am..."	80
In Memory Of Eric Ivan Burg...	82
Ode To Wreck Beach Bathers	84
If I Must Love Thee *	86
The Bus Trip Up Island	87
I'm Just Not That Pliable	88
Love In The Fair City Of Time	90
The Poet	92
When You Have Lived My Years *	93
One Lifetime Of Wandering	94
HERBERT LEIGHTON CHRISTIAN	95
Our Father A Pictured Memory	96
Our Mother Our Friend	100
CYNTHIA CHRISTIAN-BERKENBOS	101

Ode To a Seaman's Death on Losing the Q.P.R. 102

A Lady 104

I Watched Her Enter My World 105

'Twas There in the Light of the Graving Docks 106

I Beg For Your Indulgence 111

Your Ridicule Cannot Me Reach * 113

PHYLIS RINDA EBANKS 114

Definition Of A Lady... 116

I'm Waiting For The Cold To Go 116

The Water-Tight Door 118

Destructible Uncouth Despicable Man 123

Love Is Like A Speeding Bullet *... 125

Lady Death Had Called Him Home 126

Hi There Chrissy 127

Libertys 130

Where Ignorance Abounds * 131

"You Owe Me" 132

At The First Fall Of Snow 135

The Passing of Cayman's Historian 136

PERCIVAL (WILL) JACKSON 137

Hello There Dear Uncle Will 138

Power And Position * 140

Rainseeds... Like Bits Of Cotton Candy 141

Dear Reader:

To imagine horror, read "The Water-Tight Door" (page 118) how 200000 lbs of hate, neglect and ignorance cut the body of an engineer into two, which was the result of a reported defect left unrepaired because "We're losing the ship soon anyway, so let them take care of it." (The Chief Engineer's attitude at that time.)

Come along BC's Inside Passage, where you can take a "Seaman's Reprieve" (page 1) while pondering about the "White King Cruise Ship" (page 12). Enjoy the "Solid Water" (page 19) all around and feel the soft presence of the "Ferry Worker's Ghost" (page 24) as he visits the coastline among the waves. Look also at the rusting and dying relics from a time of war not long past, and of which there is no end...

You may take a look at "Man's Ignorance And Inhumanity To Men" (page 33) then seeing a nearby child, you just might see it through that child's eyes. And there is always that dream, that hopeful aspiration of finding the "Pirate's Treasure Ship Below the Pines" (page 64).

This book contains tributes to some important people in my life, who are dearly missed. I do especially want to mention here, that chief amongst these influential people, was my teacher, schoolmaster, scoutmaster and friend, Timothy E. McField (1928-1995), who had the most greatest impact on my life.

"If ye have tears to shed, prepare to shed them now." ~~M A

The Seaman's Reprieve

What for oh Boatswain I did ask
When four times four chairs were placed
Upon the rear and outer deck
Where crew alone are allowed to grace
What reason here in Granville Sound
Where the lands so closely lay
Why place these seats so uselessly
Or so at least it seemed that day

Here where the islands slight apart
Seems like in Jason's time to float
'Til but a thousand feet each side
They tower high o'er all afloat
Be it boat or ship or drifting log
Be it tug or barge or sloop
In their uninhabited wilderness
Straight to the water's edge they droop

What for oh Boatswain I did say
And his reply quick I did receive
"We place them laddie that 'ere aft
The toiling seaman may find reprieve"

The "Beaulani" Life Plan

Lift up thy mind from the mire
And thy heart will surely follow
Feed decency, trust and truth to your thoughts
That you by so doing may feed your soul
Throw off shackles of ages past and gone
Let your life be renewed and fulfilled
Cling not to norms that bound thee
For unto every life there is a reason
Even as one is snubbed out another appears
There are then but two kinds of peoples
Those who are your equals or
Those who would like to share
Let not life nor its turmoils spoil you
Let not achievements nor failures ever
Thy sweet disposition momentarily change
You are an important unique human being
Exactly what you think you are you are
No more or less than the portrait you paint of yourself
Let your reflection among others mirror
Not what they expect to see in you
But rather let your reflection be you
Let them accept the you you desire them to see
And so when necessary keep your distance
Hold fast to your genuine smile of warmth

Spread not wantonly your ideals or thoughts
'Less they be taken and against you turned
Enter then into spirits with great care
Avoiding ever their domination over you
You are responsible for your actions
Whether under the influence or not
You will have to later bear the full consequences
Therefore keep thyself above self-reproach
For in so doing you can always look
Straight into any persons eyes
You alone can condemn you
Let thy conscience then not thee accuse
You were born for a reason
You have an ultimate to fulfill
You are the maker of your destiny
One short life to live or one to kill
Take care of your ramblings
Hearts that ache alone are vulnerable
Yours is the right to seek happiness
Let its quest not from your life return
Be you best of all happy and free
Give as little or as much as you desire
Be not faint-hearted in loving
Regardless of where your affections fall
You alone must live with your decisions

You alone must face reality someday
Above all be not afraid to love
For love is the greatest happening ever
Love multiplies if shared and returns
Or bottled up rests cold and solid
Until our insides become empty and dry
Let then thy heart feed from thy mind
Think happy free and forever
You are a unique being with a purpose
Find whatever it is and cling to it ever
Let your life be loved and love be yours
For short be the time we have to spend
Then both life and love must end...

If we would live in fellowship
Then you must stay consistent
In thought -- in word -- in action
Which you upon me lay

I can but this way then appraise
As friend -- foe -- or acquaintance
As lover -- boss -- or worker
Toiling together close each day.

Hold On Jeanette Hold On

Hold on Jeanette hold on

While your voice stays tuned with Heaven

With whispers soft like angels wings

Which thru the heavenly stillness flutter

Stay by stay by Jeanette stay by

As in thoughts dreamlike I see

The visions of your loveliness

'Cross the waves brought back to me

Tarry yet tarry yet Jeanette tarry yet

Let thy presence prolong sweet sleep

Lest I open my eyes when you are gone

And no longer my dream I keep

Star gazer I in full noondays Sun

Its gleam by your radiance dimmed

Brightening shadows as you t'wards them turn

Is it real or only just seemed

Then haste thee haste Jeanette then haste

To your goal your far destiny

While like angels chorus your face and voice

Sweet will stay long in memory...

"The Cabaret Comes To Life"

Closed doors dim lights loud music
Thick smoke and high liquor smell
Then in she walks as so oft before
Her home, her heaven in to dwell
Crowded floors scarce of seats
Arthur Murray's students so stiff
Waltz across the glossy wooden floor
Black metallic rails a border makes
Liquor orders for the barmaid
An unsmiling distant waitress takes
And the music blares forth
Deadening, deafening, distracting
Leading you into realms of wonder
As once more the Cabaret comes to life.

The old accustomed country band
Blares out its 'stand by me' tune
While the leader drones the lyrics
The drummer softly like moonstruck dog
Barks in back unintelligibly in a moan
Then the floor shakes and trembles
As the dancers who did there congregate
Changes from their slow easy shuffle
As the tempo changes to a stomping beat

And wild Disco moods prevail
Saturday night fever is felt
As each pair tries to imitate
The dancers from some filmstrip scene
Wire brush against the pigskin drumhead
Wail of organ like cat in heat
Cymbals banging... Trumpet out of tune
All conglomerate into a confusion
A confusion with an indiscernible beat
Yet a confusion which-to to move your feet
As the madness hits young and old
Leading them into new realms of wonder
As the excitement of the Cabaret comes to life.

Then what seems lifelike like silence
A space wherein one can at least for a moment
Hear themselves clear think
The screaming waitress can now ask
Do you want another drink?
Conversations tidbits linger in the air
Lone men and women wander on
Each seeking an opposite with to pair
A drink a dance or mayhap
A night together they to share
Each alone yet wary of the other

Afraid to let their hidden feelings out
So back instead to another drink
A few choice thoughts for the next song
A hope or plan to set in motion
When the band returns to stage from its break
When the music again will shelter
When behind the noise and turmoil
Once again they can enter the realm of wonder
Whispering desires aloud and uncaring
As they rest protected from reality
Because the great Cabaret has come back to life

Stay awhile miss another drink or two
No more beer yes then a gin will do
Take care buddy watch where you step
Sorry, no man why should we fight
Legs scramble fastly noisily away
That's right let's just enjoy tonight
Sorry Hon I'm with this chick here
See you next week alone okay
But careful now say no more
Why spoil and upset an evening
Here have another drink on me
Then meet me for a quick hug and kiss
Yes around the corner is fine

And remember the next dance is mine
Touch lightly on the floor so knowingly
As two hookers give me looks impatiently
Don their coats and finish their drinks
Grab their significant black bags
Hustle to the door alone and mad
Another place to visit and a try to make
Just too many women around tonight
Too many women lonely and available
Three to each lone male on the beat
Disrupts any chance of a value sale
As the band returns to stage with a song
And the jukebox suddenly goes silent
While the first rush of dancers re-appear
Once more they wait for the bands last stand
Paired off are they hand in welcome hand
Losing themselves in the realms of wonder
Ecstatic that the dance floor of the Cabaret
Again has come to life...

If you be wrong admit it and correct it
If you be right defend it and leave all compromise to those who live spineless.

*MAY GOD ALWAYS KEEP YOU SAFE
IN HIS TENDER LOVING CARE
ALWAYS IN OUR MEMORIES
FOREVER IN OUR HEARTS*

A Treasure Deeply Missed
ISABEL ALICE CHRISTIAN WASHINGTON
January 27, 1954 - February 1, 2016

Remembered fondly by your siblings:
Eugene Leighton, Dudley Noel, Clive Anthony,
Barbara Mary, Molly-Ann Amelda, and Marion Margaret,
and your children: Ricky and Victoria.

Borning Of A Day

Once in a while we all should ponder
The borning of a day
As the Golden Sun another day begins
A new day one uniquely yours
In so many many ways
The mountains darkness underneath
The wisps of morning clouds
All come to Golden life anew
As natures light all they enshroud
The ripples soft on waters calm
Broken by splash of jumping fish
As the mornings Sun creeps
Up from its sleep
A new dawn a new wish
A new day just to contemplate
As the morning is being born
What lies ahead each of us for
Which anew we'll start this morn
What mark will make we on life's highway
Before start of tomorrow's dawn
Once in a while we all should ponder
The borning of a day
As the Golden Sun another day begins
A new day one uniquely yours
In so many many ways

Legend Of The Lost "White King" Cruise Ship...

'Twas a cold dark damp July eve
E'en with the clouds hanging low
'Til it seemed the trees without a top
Higher than the sky above did grow
The swish swash splash of water fell
Like demons from each waves crest
And like a maiden's moan afar off
It screamed long and soft to itself
The life of engines whining deep
As they strained to keep ahead
Were like moans of men on battlefields
Like moans of the living dead
Then a wisp of cloud it broke anew
To a path 'cross the waters show
While the howling wind 'cross the waves
Screamed like the mythical shrew
'Twas such an eve I remember well
When the White King ship set sail
Through the fjord-like passage waterways
Through those mountain-clad waterways
Where the clouds hung low enough to touch
Where the chills of winter stays
Where the killer whales in frolic fun

Off the seas cascade and play.
'Twas a cold dark dismal July eve
With the lightships light off beam
Where one saw their tired piercing eye
Thru the fog bound mist dim gleam
And the pure white head of the Eagle bald
Perched high upon the limb
'Twas the only moving nature life
Seen as the White King sailed by him
One felt for reason yet unknown
That the time it was at hand
One wondered at the many souls
Happy in full shared vacation plan
So full of mirth and confidence
When on their ship they came
To seek to fill their lifelong dreams
Then thru these Straights return again
Return to where the Sun warm shone
Return to cloudless open skies
Where fjord mountains killer whales
Were but pictures they would prize
And the White King ship sailed on
Fast on towards their destinies
No serious thought to the dark clouds given

Which hung so low over land and sea.
'Twas a fork, a Y point in the route
Where it seemed the mountains met
That the skipper left the course he knew
And up the other route course set
Was it to the pink painted tug avoid
Which it two North Arm barges towed
Laden with construction accoutrements
Straining heavily 'neath its load
Was it to perhaps an hour change
Or a clearer fogless path to go
Did the Coast Guard he a warning give
Why he changed we'll never know
Yet tho the evening Sun had set
Still the dark was not complete
And off to Port twix ship and land
Few white Seagulls clear were seen
Then a hundred yards offshore we were
Sometimes a hundred feet or less
Still only faint foreboding and so dark
Of the shoreline could they attest
For the clouds of grey hung over all
Enfolding land and ship and man
Cutting off their visual contact with

Guiding marks and lights on land
Still the White King ship sailed on
Her creamy white sides all agleam
With faces which thru portholes peeked
Lost in the still pleasures of their dreams
And the evenings Suns bright disappeared
While lower yet the dark clouds hung
Making smaller with each moment past
The space of sight which to they clung

And the vastness of the grey dark void
Like a threatening nightmare lay
O'ershadowing fast their traveled route
Blanking out their proposed way
And the waters fell from the last waves crest
With its splish splash swish and sway
While the demon-like moans mixed with pain
From some poor dying lips soft play
Still the engines moaned in tired response
Giving of their power the best
And the adults partied on the White King ship
While the kids were laid to rest
Six hundred souls had set a-sail
On that last ill-fated ride

Which on a cold wet dark July day
Had glided o'er the tide
From a jetty where the fish boats rest
By the pilings fresh being driven
As the Greenleaf Piledriver clunked
Its metallic tattoo on wood being driven

Such a day it was when she set out
While a freighter grey aft passed
Showing green its normal undersides
Empty now, lifted high, moving fast
Then the bank of fog waited playfully
Like an actor's help for curtain call
'Til the White King ship on its stage was set
Then it let its blanketing curtain fall
As the diesels hummed their endless song
And the waters splished and splashed
The moaning waves and the crying wind
Echoed thru the riggings stashed
'Twas a dismal day the White King sailed
Like an omen it remains
Tho the waters now are strangely still
'Cross it drifts those sounds again
Of waters splish splash swash and swish

Of the laboured moans of engines deep
Of the cry of women labouring yet
Of pain like men seeking deaths release
Of the sirens song which so oft will drift
Of the demon-like banshees shriek
Of the call of six hundred lost souls
In full unison for help they seek
Yet it never came far as we know
Least not from mortal hand
For the White King took that fjord route
Nevermore to be seen by man
Off somewhere 'tween living and dead
In the unknown her fate remains
Not a spar, a call, a raft nor rope
No signs whatever of her pains
Yet it's known by those who sail the seas
That jetsam and flotsam will e'er tell
Of the end of all which on it float
Brought clear by tides ebb and swell
Still tho the years have come and quickly gone
Tho the waters searched have been
Not a message of ship living or dead
Came from those women and those men
Yet upon occasion in the eve

When the fog a thick blanket lays
When the clouds come down treetops around
When the charted course is sailed
Oft times one see the huge silhouette
Of the White King making turn
Into a course where no water lay
Silent dark distant moving on
Still to follow close would disaster be
For its sheer tall mountainside
Which stands before the White King ship
As on her new found course she rides
Still as the silhouette passes by
E'en when it's calm and the wind is still
One can hear the splish splash of waters fall
Like demons call from the waveless crest
And like the maidens moan off so far off
Still the engines whine is clearly heard
As like but the White King cruisers knew
Yet the secret course remains unknown
Which from the Inside Passage she took
Another mystery held of the cold cold deep
Another entry in the Seas log book.

Solid Water... Solid Water...

Solid water solid water
Not icy nor frozen yet solid
I do declare it must be solid
The water which below us lie
As ships float o'er and boats pass by
As waves do toss and turn us high
That water must be solid
How else could so much bulk of steel
Rise high on wave to pitch and wheel
Then off the crest is tossed you feel
Yet rights itself upon its keel
Unless that's solid water
Like children happy in winters time
Tobogganing down the mountain side
First to climb up then down slide
The base of solid earth they ride
The soft snows like waves don't hinder
So once again in deep thought say I
That surely as safe the ship doth ride
Pitched and tossed on the waves to slide
Below the crest a base must hide
A base... aye a base of solid water
Solid water... solid water
Not icy nor frozen yet solid
Solid water... solid water
I do declare it must be solid water...

Earthchild... Behind Your Eyes...

Behind your laughing smiling eyes
A secret hid deep you keep
A vision past of what has been
Which haunts e'en yet your sleep
A thought of times long gone and been
When in another time you knew
Happier moments filled with joy
Plans of lasting love ever true
And yet you've ne'er lost your warmth
Which with your smile is filled
Your happy bright outlook at life
Making life with you a thrill
To see the vibrant tones you own
Go out this place to bright
To warm and fill life's emptiness
Making again the world seem right
Your call by nature natural is
Since an Earthchild you've remained
A builder of life's Universe
A part small but total just the same
The secrets of creation lie
Deep within your body hidden
Tho dormant they may present lay
Their fulfillment for you've striven

That's why tho time may cruel be
In time its scars will heal
To better yet our paths prepare
That we with life may deal
Then once again a year beckons
Stop ponder think and plan
One year is past another calls
To relive change or just let stand
Each day the tides change on the seas
Each month the moon renews
Each quarter new a season gives
Each year once to change our views
So Earthchild stop upon your day
Step out awhile and clearer see
Your past as past tho beautiful
Your present and future free
Then grasp the life life's given you
And in mind thought and body stay
Happy full in heart all year thru
Like on this your special day
May joy and peace and contentedness
Forever your life with be blessed
Luck patience and good fortune too
Friendships warm and happiness
Then when your new day dawneth

Your new Sun brightly shines
May in your world enter lasting love
The kind you've sought to find
May your new years each one find you
Waiting for them anxiously
A pathway they to new pedestals high
New visions wherefrom to see
Last may you live but to enjoy
Just one more Birthday than the last
On endlessly as true eternity
More fulfilled each than those past.

When you were born
the Doctor proclaimed to your Parent/s...
"You are the Mother/Father
of a Beautiful baby BOY/GIRL."
... so now, where the Hell did the idea of
YOUR having/making a GENDER CHOICE get
into YOUR distorting the TRUTH?/FACTS...?

© 1972

The Ghostlike Moon...

Like a ghost behind a cloud it lay
With its eerie searching beam
Flashing on and off off and on
Selected spots only on it seems
Then a large black grey white mass
Shadowed o'er what we could view
Making of itself shadow pictures high
Backgrounded with spots of blue
A blue buoy marker in channel flash
And in response so quick appears
Once more so ghost like and serene
The soft late spring moon half there
Then as one glances up it's gone
Behind another cloud to seek refuge
As it trips so light and playfully
O'er the mountains -- oceans -- woods
Like a ghost behind the clouds it lies
Like a florescent cool light beam
But by mornings tide tho clouds are gone
No more will its light be seen
Like a ghost a ghost a haunting ghost
It comes and goes unheard
Passing soft unfelt o'er all the land
Like a ghost with ne'er a word...

Legend Of The Ferry Worker's Ghost

In the lift I feel his presence
On the stairs I hear his feet
In the dark and lonesome corner
I can see his face a-peek
In the cabin where he once lay
Oft one sees the cabin door
Ope' when no one else is present
Indent his bunk so soft once more
It the eve there still drifts laughter
Which to him was so unique
Cut so short and still at midnight
When one hears him softly speak
Thru the halls and thru the alleys
Eerie distant moans and screams
As in death he walks among us
As he did in life and dreams...
Lean and lanky he in stature
Tall with flowing golden hair
Blue of eyes and bronze complexioned
Slow to anger, hate, despair
So he lived and worked unnoticed
By the many that he knew
Just another fellow sailor

Spending life upon the blue
Yet within his breast deep hidden
Held he love for one who called
Small and frail swanlike she beckoned
She to him his one and all
Far away across the waters
She on other tides did care
Planning ever for their future
When life together they could share
Soft and blond with blue eyes shining
In a face with life so filled
Lips like rosebuds slightly opened
Which for him were never chilled
Fate itself worked them it seemed for
When his ship at last made stay
Close besides her ship it berthed
Had not time to spend together they
Spring had come into his Winter
Summers warmth thruout the year
Seasons all blossomed with roses
Fragrant paths theirs everywhere
And they frolicked in their pleasures
Happy carefree so in love
Dreaming of the long shared future
Which within their grasp seemed now

Warmly thru the soft snows of winter
Side by side in love they stayed
Sharing all the Season's Greetings
No thought they to be afraid
Winter passed and Spring had broken
Blossoms with the trees were filled
Birds sought new nests for their roosting
Life anew o'er nature spilled
But fate changed their preparations
Calling out him again to sea
Soon to return at end of fortnight
To warm love awaiting patiently
Back renewed while destiny waited
Silent Gloomy Full of Despair
How best now could it their unity
Tear asunder and it share
Smile of evil thoughts a-thinking
Laughter low of dismal plan
Visioning their sudden parting
Destiny waited for that man
Out to work like often before
Moving sprightly here and there
Chances which before he'd taken
Once more chanced without a care

Happy he too happy surely
Ever to disaster call
Let the safety rope hang loosely
Ne'er before did he e'er fall
O'er the side he washed and painted
Suspended there on scaffold line
Swinging happy in his labours
Singing softly 'till lunchtime
Now his shipmates joke and rib him
Now they leave him working 'lone
Now he sees Fate stand before him
Unrecognized... Silent... Alone
The chilling hands reach out to touch him
The breath of destiny he feels
His scaffold rope Fate quietly loosens
He aghast now scarcely breathes
Then the echoes of his singing
In his ears again he hears
And the tune he whistled softly
Re-echoes loudly into his ears
Faces flash with passing fury
As his past is all recalled
'Til but stands her face before him
Fate thereat the rope let fall

Realization fills his vocals
As for seconds three he screams
'Til the fishplate near the water
Ends forevermore his dreams
Echo -- Echo -- Still it echoes
As his shipmates his body bare
Dead he floated there beneath them
Gone too quick to offer prayer
So his body they watch buried
Then again they put to sea
But his memory ghostlike lingers
Here where once walked happy he
And back home his love still beckons
Swanlike silent she remains
She alone rejects his passing
Waits for him to come again

Is she then wrong in her waiting
Does she contact with him hold
Who can answer full that question
Of love which reaches past deaths door
Yet it's said at times it's silent
When she to his old ship comes
And on her face a smile will linger
As his whistle to her comes

But often at the turn of evening
Same the time they last did spend
One can hear his voice soft speaking
Cut soon short by screams of pain
On the ferry where he laboured
Filled his space has so long been
Yet he walks the self-same spaces
Sits in fellowship with the men
You may meet him by your cabin
Or upon the deck he walked
Or perhaps he's at your table
That extra voice you're hearing talk
When you hear him don't you panic
Speak to him and call him friend
He in spirit e'er will sail here
Seeking but to live again

In the lift I feel his presence
On the stairs I hear his feet
In the dark and lonesome corner
I can see his face a-peek...

The Mortal Man's Approach

Without a word or reason
Without a formal note or call
Up-walking to her straight he said
"Madam I do fully intend
To wrap myself within your arms
Entangle myself within thy hair
Be enveloped by your fragrance sweet
While I feed to satisfaction
My wishes hungers and desires
From among the many delights
Which before me you expose
Cherry lips mine for the tasting
'Tween two rosy appled cheeks
In a face like ripe peaches
Mixed with sweet sweet cream
A bosom like the hawthorns
White flowers it is spread
Beneath a milky shoulder small petit
Swanlike and like apparitions
Long slender fingers call to me
Ever close and ever-closer
'Til I hear your laughter sweet
Cascade like rippling waters
From distant mountains-side

All the while your sweet breath
Gives life anew to my dying body all
Steadfast with love and beauty
Like the early evenings stars
In a sky of azure blue
Now turned into snowy white
So your smiling eyes me they welcome
Call silently yet constant
Unto my heart yours from to come sup
How then could I mere mortal
Refuse thy angels call
Resist the charms from heaven
Which the universe thee has willed
Why then should I the hungry
Turn away from feast to fasting
Let all thy delights so exposed
Be forevermore lost to me
No fool am I tho mortal
Nor dimwitted cold not stupid
As man or God would have to be
Thy offers to refuse
Thus here I stand before thee
One step from earthly heaven
But feasting first mine eyes
'Fore tasting all that's thine."

Prepare thyself I tell me
For long has she prepared
'Til nothing now on her
Is wanting nor unseen
Fear not the charms about her
These are but appetizers
Until you reach those treasures
Far too fit for a king

"Then lady hear my tribute
Tho in mind only soft spoken
Its clarity is visible
In these eyes which worship thee
Take warning what I tell true
For no other shall be offered
As you in my arms enfold I now
To complete my plans for thee
I take you as I told you
I wrap entangle and envelope
And here I shall remain
Until my life is cut short
Or no more delights in thee I see..."

Man's Ignorance And Inhumanity To Men...

As my ship pulls so slowly out of harbour
Tho the rain is falling I can see
The relics of our long past generations
Which in our warring men put out to sea
I can hear within my thoughts again the echoes
As the sister ships of these set out a-sail
Only soon to plunge towards the oceans bottom
As torpedoes to avoid they all did fail

I can vision all the cries and all the sorrows
Which aboard those fatal ships its sailors knew
I can hear them plead aloud and beg for mercy
Praying that the nightmare hell would soon be thru
But the agony and pain it just continued
Having done to them what they'd set out to do
Yes their agony and Pain it continued
Having done to them what they'd set out to do

Now it's years and generations after
And in fellowship their enemies are friend
But those sleeping in their salty graves forever
Never knew nor ever will know of its end
So I alone can only stand and ponder
What went thru the minds of all those long dead men
As I gaze with sorrow at these grim reminders
Of man's ignorance an' inhumanity to men

I recall the years about which all are written
Telling full the story over without fail
Of the reasons given which they went and died for
Reasons all which now seem to no avail
All the rapture and the dangers and enticements
All the lies the force which sent them over there
Just to suffer and to give their lives so useless
Killing foreign fellow humans without care

Dying in the snows and in the muds of Europe
Dying in the hope to one day set men free
Yet themselves sent out to kill unwilling
No succour nor reprieve in their country
Grim reaper he of life had a full harvest
For those years as worldwide blood did flow
As man strove abroad to others kill in battle
While at home those profiting watched him go

Then after all the shells and all the mortars
Had all fallen silent there remained
Just these rusting rotting relics as mementos
Of man's ignorance 'n' inhumanity to men
Just these rusting rotting relics as mementos
Of mankind's ignorance and inhumanity to men

Yet it goes on and on and on forever
Never ceasing in their ways of making war

Building more and more and greater killing weapons
Never having learnt from the wars before
Then within my breast there is a tremor
As my overbearing heart a shudder gives
While my blood reboils and my anger rises
Against those who would start it all again
There is nothing left here then but my visions
As again I gaze across the rainy sea
To those rusting rotting wrecked reminders
Of the past war makers such as these
But alas my feeble voice but one is
In a world of turmoil shouts and noise
And my thoughts can but travel back again yet
To those men so young upon those relics poised

Then as my ship pulls slowly out of harbour
I can hear anew their screams and cries of pain
As so many good men died to keep watch
O'er man's mementos of his cruelty to men
As the wind blows o'er the empty deck plates
The waters lap thru hulls and then to shore
But if you listen closely to their mournings
They are pleading "leave reminders nevermore"
Ever pleading o'er the old mementos
Cease inhumanities to man we do implore
Ever pleading o'er the old mementos
Cease inhumanities to man we thee implore

Skygazing...

In deep and pensive mood I lay

Skygazing

While Sunworshippers on the beach around

Are lazing

The wind is calm

The Sun is hot

The water cool inviting

Yet still in pensive mood I lie

Skygazing

Across the lake on distant shore

A-flashing

A motor's noisy thump and ride

Come thumping

The kids are screaming

Radios loud beaming

Wet bodies lie gleaming

Yet in deep pensive mood lie I

Skygazing

Wavelets form across the lake

Retreating

Partiers on the lakeshore all

Are drinking

Towels many now are spread
Air pillow and blanket bed
With bathers lying burnt and red
Still pensive without a word I lie
Skygazing
No need have I the time to spend
Sunbathing
For with tan forever I am blessed
Unchanging
So while they in the Sun will lay
I lie and ponder deep the day
Content we each in our own way
While in deep and pensive mood I stay
Skygazing
No clouds no rain just azure blue
Unending
No break or stay within my view
Restricting
So as the birds and crickets sings
Across the lake the laughter rings
You in the warm Sun do your thing
While in the shade pensively content
I lay... Skygazing.

The Shrew Of The Inside Passage

Hiss hiss hiss and strike
Demon-like with banshee voice
Shrill pitched screams and fangs
Tearing down devouring endlessly
So appears the Shrew of the Inside Passage
The shrew who makes life miserable
The shrew who causes so many jobs
The shrew who rules nowhere really
Yet the shrew who thinks she should
Waiting like a snake in the grass
Like a bat after blood in the night
Like a wolf for the innocent lamb
Each time waits the shrew for her prey
By her screech and scream you see her
By her newsy nose upheld you find
That deceit and slurs are her weapons
As so cunningly she enters your mind
There she plays your friend at being
'Til your plans and secrets she knows
Now in her grasp you she will strangle
If you straight her way do not go
And the Shrew sails the Inside Passage
Content to just lie there in wait
Intent it seems life to make harried

For someone new each trip she takes
She the shrew her voice like a demon
She with screech like banshees shrill
Waiting but for her tongue to loosen
Waiting spirits on new to kill
Like an old hen she feels she's the ruler
The Work area like a barnhouse her roost
Keeping those chicks which do full her bidding
So quickly all others cut she loose
But the young chicks wait on in silence
One day soon her cluck-clucking to end
When she stands plucked of her feathers
Look around she will be seeking a friend
But they all will then grimly remember
Their terms of work cut so short she did
Of the hassles backbiting and gossip
She spread if they did not her bid
And reject the Shrew of the Inside Passage ...

Reject they the shrew who made life miserable
Reject they the shrew who caused so many jobs
Reject they the shrew who rules nowhere really
Reject they the shrew who thinks that she should
Reject they the shrew the Shrew of the Inside Passage

Friend... Aye He Is One...

He was raised in a circus he said
Yet he was not a circus freak
More a blessed one touched by nature
Impeded so slight he in speech
Taught by some of the lower of men
The baser of women and life
He grew to despise in disappointment
His home his culture his life
For they like an animal untended
Had food and shelter him given
But held back e'en basic education
A necessity grim just for living
Still nature takes care of her own
The worst gifted to she somehow atones
For of friends he had more than a few
Which gave him daily strength to go on
In the reaches of circus his living
He'd eked out as barker for years
Laying in solemn moments after
His insides awash with his tears
Yet the code of his life stood firmly
What makes every clown wear a smile
It's learning to control all emotions

It's learning you never can cry
By this token he grew and existed
Just a part of a wandering band
Seeing life among the more fortunate
He like beggar living to mouth from hand
Yet within him a current was moving
As he determined his best yet to be
So he quit the touring of circus
Joined he the tours of the sea
He was slow in the knowledgeable matters
He was restricted positions to hold
But his love of life and its peoples
Made him endeared to all like fine gold
He a heart had as big as a mountain
To complain he didn't physically see
What would cause him duty to leave waiting
Would in pain cause five men to flee
No toil to would he stand rejecting
'Fore asked for his help he would lend
He to any and all who did meet him
He left with warm smile like a friend
In his playful old chorus of barkers
His voice a caution out would ring
To insure his movements unhampered

Would no one injure, restrict or offend
Versatile as the changes of weather
Which above all the sun constant shines
So his face in the grimmest situation
With an eye twinkle would break into smile
To con you never would he try
Tho a salesman himself of he was
With a warranty no business can offer
It's done right or over it he does
Tho like many I knew awhile short
Yet on me an impression he made
For this child blessed he by nature
Gave back more than life to him gave
When you meet him at sea in your travels
Stop you awhile and ponder the thought
This man without education bare formal
Has learnt he to live as men ought
He was raised in a circus he told me
Now he a living is making at sea
Spreading love joy and helpful devotion
A true picture, he, of humanity.

(A tribute to BC Ferry co-worker "Ivan")

The Morning's Softness...

As the morning clouds

Rest their cotton softness

Against the mountains top

The trees seem to cry out in sweet refrain

As the morning stillness

Remains unbroken yet

The silent winged eagle

With meal secured in claws

Heads for its nest again

As the glimmering mornings sunshine

Removes the foggy haze

Revealing full the beauty of the day

One can but pause in awe

And deep appreciation of it all

As the ripples break the waters

With their glassy liquid rolls

And the first sounds of the day is heard

As we listen to the shrill sweet sounds

Of a birds distant mating call

Then the world awakes to noises

Then the world in movement toils

Then the peaceful stillness of the morning

It is gone

Youth... With Your Eyes You Flatter Me

With your eyes
How sweet you flatter me
But why inflate my ego
Why spread my confidence
'Round dreams I dare not hold
Your youth and beauty
Fair and rare entreat me
Reach out and touch awhile
This vision offered now
Yet in my thoughts I ponder
Can this real be and if
Can this then last unchanged
If so what price I pay
What exchange must I give
To hold this dream you offer
Which flatter now and thrill me
This dream I watch your eyes in
When I behold your face
When I long for but just once
Your cherry lips to taste
But shall I do so to destruction
Shall I thy charms fall for
Shall I envelope in my arms
Your body lithe and warm
So filled with vibrance and with youth
Shall I thy offers take sincere

As honest genuine full of truth
Or just a play of youth's time
A recall to see an old fool fall
To dangle heaven 'fore my eyes
Then to refuse me all

Fear not now for thy heart
The soul or body that is yours
These crave I not to harm
Nor yet to use and cast aside
But only once to now be held close
To feel your warmth around me
To be enveloped in your arms
To render thoughts hereafter
Of the ecstasy we have shared
This then is why I flatter thee
This alone is why you to I call
No game nor deceit do I hold
No pinnacle wherefrom to see you fall
Can this be real as read
Is true these words I'm hearing
Is youth so filled with wisdom now
To mean what eyes are saying
Perhaps my mind is weary
Like my heart by age it's dimmed
I vision what I want to see
In your eyes see what I long to hear

This then is but fickle fates charade
To parade youth my eyes before
To see me reach and try to grasp
Then laugh as I fall once more
So flat upon my face
Then haste thee fate and youth
Find other life to a mockery make
Find other fool this game to play
Find other heart again to break
For mine too oft has shattered been
You youth with eyes a-calling
Such flattery you transpose
Across the reaches of my mind
Into my very soul
If only I could reach the realm
Of life whereon the future stands
Then of the promises your eyes give
I would reach out for as man
Alas destruction waits for me
My years since last my youth
Which spent has been in upwards toil
Now face me with their truth
Youth is not gone from out of life
It's where it's always been
What's gone is strength to start anew
Letting go of what has been
Fate life oft time calls upon

To renew and rejuvenate
By parading youth before the eyes
Of those who of life contemplates
Thus as with your eyes
Me you flatter sweet
My confidence spreads, ego inflates
I rest yet back experience upon
Next move still yours to make
For tho my arms ache for you
My lips hunger for you kiss
Your youthful form inviting soft
So near to me it is

Yet it's your move youth of today
Tho here resistance you won't find
As I in patience here shall sit
Your world awaiting to enter mine

A word soft spoke
A touch of hand
A call to alone with you
A message write so secretly
Then with you youth
I'll gladly share loves rendezvous...

Dip... Dip... Dip And Dive...

Dip dip dip and dive
You grey white vision in the sky
Flip flip flap and flip
'Til your wings push you ever higher
Stop stop stop and soar
Glide on current high of air
Bead-like eyes webbed folded feet
Appear then disappear
Gone awhile as drizzle falls
Soft upon the quiet deck
Far away like silhouette
Aft against the clouds you stay
Now upon another breeze
Fast towards us you glide
Dip and dive dip and dive
There's food upon the tide
Grey above and at your tips
Pure snow white below
Was it to from Sun's rays protect
That nature painted you so
What propels you heavier than air
As so soft you fly
Flip of wing nod of head
Then fast forward steady glide

Now your landing gear descend
But short to slow your flight
As you survey all below
From you lofty vantage point
Bird of class and beauty you
Whom for kiss of seas they named
You who fly so near untouched
By the highest of waves sprayed
You in splendour being gazed at
By old and young at sea
As you cavort in playful flight
An emblem of the free
Fly then far outwards out above
Fly then but stay and rest
Your beauty and your majesty
Which our presence with, you bless
I sat and watched a seagull fly
Across the briny seas
Now here then gone
Now near then on
Dip dip dip dip
Dip dip dip and dive
Across the briny sea...

The Artist Nature

Green gossamer waters
Reflective of tall wavy pines
Cut like a bald headed person
From its plateau-like mountainside
Birds skim along swiftly
As fishing boats hug the shore
Current swells move obviously
Tossing twirling logs abroad
Faint glimmer of sunshine
Faint drizzle from scattered clouds
Spots of liquid blue in the heavens
Dark fluffy cumulus around
Like the painting of an artist
Yet ever changing ne'er the same
Just like frames in movie making
Each one different yet the same
Isles of wonder uninhabited
By save but few of natures wild
In the background smoke arises
From some lone prospectors pile
Ah! There's the faintest glimmer
Of the artists natures palette
As he fashions seven colours
Into a glimmer of rainbows wet

Now the rainbow has been copied
As upon the waves crest appears
Seven rainbows following each other
Making their indentations on the waves
Spotlite like a beam of radiance
Touches full and lights in blaze
Yonder island by its lonesome
Glimmering shores across the waves
Now the beam of sunlight changes
Rests on another of life's stage
As like in telescopic grandeur
A tug small fills the moment's page
Click click click of camera lenses
Spot of nature held secure
On a wonder bit of filmstrip
As nature moves her spotlight on
Ah! The artist nature truly
Has a way with paints and props
As his lights rest on each subject
Awhile enhancing yet never stops.

Tho long I may woo you passionately
Yet never will I crawl nor to thee beg.

Granville Channel

Lake-like the sea became
As the distance closed behind us
As the towering mountains rose
Straight from the oceans floor
Their green pine covered footings
Their snow-capped covered tops
With here and there a clearing
Where the growth of trees were stopped
Ahead again they thunder high
No passage visible you see
Land locked we feel and so appear
Land locked on an open sea
The salty spray falls on your face
Its briny taste it is sweet
Bring back you to the present
With all its grim realities
Aside a barge is bucking waves
Like an overladen pack horse
As abit ahead tugs engines scream
To keep that barge on course
The waves splash and play upon its bow
Like a cat with ball of twine
Showing man its powers yet unleashed

A cautious word him to remind
Then rainy mist blanks out the sun
As a plane drones overhead
Twin Otter on its rescue run
'Fore the sea can claim its dead
A fishing boat then two now three
Their long booms out overside
The long hooked lines trip playfully
O'er the wavelets wash and tide
And still we move and yet we seem
As tho on a land locked lake we be
As boom of logs still topped with snow
Passes by chained but drifting free
The lumber mill the logger's camp
The barge laden with mobile homes
Then the mountains seem to separate
Restrict our outbound route no more
Still again the sea lake-like becomes
When around the bend we weave
Mountains in majestic beauty picturesque
Scenes we see and hate to leave.

The Northwind...

Cold she blows so cold
Aye so cold she blows
Her cold and wintry breath
Chillingly falls across the sea
The clouds hang loose
The trees sway lightly
While along the bright shoreline
Sunworshippers bare their backs
Only to shiver in surprise
For unsuspectingly she blows
Aye so cold she blows
Her cold and wintry breath
Falls chillingly o'er the sea
But stay pause awhile and ponder
What time and season now of year
This be, surely not spring is it
Nay spring has come and gone
Its flowers they have given way
To fruit where fragrant blossoms lay
Perhaps then Fall upon us is and early
How could this be when fruit still
Upon the trees fresh stay
When grapes await their harvest
Sweet purple on the vine

Is this then truly Summer time
Certainly you mock the time
Or mayhap mother nature
Another quirk has planned
Why else would blow she so cold
So cold her Wintry feeling breath
So cold upon the sunlit beach
So chillingly across the glistening sea
Far north far north too far north
Where Winter's solstice never wanes
Where snows melt not in season
Far north where trees, flowers, plants
Enjoy life anew without true warmth
Where sunlight falls but isn't felt
Where frozen lakes they never melt
Where man and fish and bird adapt
To lives of sub-zero Celsius
And on the land the hills and trees
And on the ships the beach and seas
She blows so cold so cold she blows
Aye the northwind cold she blows.

Persona Mea...

Like a fallen cross
Upon the fresh cut Summer grass I lay
My face uplifted
Gazing at the vast expanse of universe
Thoughts like the birds in flight
Flutter across the reaches of my mind
My brain like the covering clouds
A grey blanket of overshadowing cover
While life goes on below
The steady movement
Of automobiles on the paved highway
The sounds of children and of pets
Laughing and barking in full merriment
The rustle of leaves on trees
Blown playfully about the supporting limb
As the sun slowly sinks
Leaving another long grey shadow behind
While life goes on below
The chirp of a bush cricket
Its shrill whistle cuts sharply and across
A songbird's tune falls soft
Yet its full refrain is distinguishable
The man made noises loud
Still cannot drown the sounds of nature

The trickle of the stream
As across the pebbles smooth it flows
Joins in musical harmony
Enveloped tho they be under shades of grey
While life goes on below
Still soft lie I uplooking
My arms outstretched like a fallen cross
My mind a whirl of thoughts
As thru it passes all the thoughts of time
I am a part of this
A small and maybe insignificant seeming part
But none the less a part
A necessary tidbit to form part of a whole
This then is why the universe is
This then is why I am and must remain
While life goes on here below.

> My part of my life
> that is my life is my life
> but is your part of your life
> that is your life your life... ?

"The Fool Felt Duty Bound"...

The fool felt duty bound entrapped
NO respite for his sentence stood
Content he to for his folly ever pay
'Til parting death release bring to him would

Then dawned the late springs month
When Sunshine fell upon his face in warmth
When Mays showers had not yet a-washed
The fragrance sweet of flowers that yet lay

'Twas then the fool 'woke with a start
Surely it's some other to the voice it speaks
Soft sweet like angels call from off afar
Promises such life which of he daren't seek

COME WITH ME RUN AWAY AND LIVE
COME BE THE ONE THAT I HAVE WAITED FOR
COME HOLD ME TENDER TO THYSELF
COME LET ME BE YOUR EVERMORE ADORED

The fool felt duty bound entrapped
No release from his chains saw he
How could he loose the bands which bound
How could he heed the call and be free

Can life be real when lived in prison walls
When soul is empty and heart lives in pain
While body fast is held by duty bound
As mind and spirit lives but to hear again

COME WITH ME RUN AWAY AND LIVE
COME BE THE ONE THAT I HAVE WAITED FOR
COME HOLD ME TENDER TO THYSELF
COME LET ME BE YOUR EVERMORE ADORED

To hear within the very soul those words
As trembling lips plead back answering
Don't tempt me please don't tempt me
'Fore o'er the brink of emptiness I spring.

The fool still duty bound remained
Alone within the loneliness he lives
Afraid perhaps the call in jest was made
Afraid to lose if again his heart he gives

COME WITH ME RUN AWAY AND LIVE
COME BE THE ONE THAT I HAVE WAITED FOR
COME HOLD ME TENDER TO THYSELF
COME LET ME BE YOUR EVERMORE ADORED

If these words genuine and true remains
Give but one sign unto now the fool
Let the soul and heart feel it may last
Let not your words be words of jest so cruel

A fool that's bound in deep nothingness
Will grasp a breath for of fresh air
Will gamble all but for loves caress
Will blindly leave and run out anywhere

COME WITH ME RUN AWAY AND LIVE
COME BE THE ONE THAT I HAVE WAITED FOR
COME HOLD ME TENDER TO THYSELF
COME LET ME BE YOUR EVERMORE ADORED

Alas the fool that's duty bound awaits
A word or gesture from the voice that calls
Alive again the spirit in him seems
As breathlessly he wishes for the call

One call collect his time to ensure
Once more the voice inviting but to hear
Then short the hours trapped will he endure
'Fore reaching out the caller to hold near

Cast off the caution and the bands
Cast off the hurt wherein he's bound
New life enveloping he as man
His heart in love song bursting out in sound

THE FOOL A FOOL NO MORE AND FREE
WITH WORD RENEWED TO HIM SO SOFTLY GIVEN
LIKE MAN ALIVE AGAIN WHO ONCE WAS DEAD
REACHES UP TO THE VOICE
STRAIGHT OUT OF HEAVEN

I'LL COME AND RUN AWAY AND LIVE
I'LL BE THE ONE WHOM YOU HAVE WAITED FOR
LONG I TO HOLD YOU TENDER TO MYSELF
EVERMORE YOU THE ONE THAT THE FOOL ADORE.

The fool felt duty bound -- entrapped
No respite for his sentence stood
Content he to for his folly ever pay
'Til parting death release bring to him would

Then dawned the late springs month
When sunshine fell upon his face in warmth
When Mays showers had not yet a-washed
The fragrance sweet of flowers that yet lay...

THE FOOL A FOOL NO MORE AND FREE
WITH WORD RENEWED TO HIM SO SOFTLY GIVEN
LIKE MAN ALIVE AGAIN WHO ONCE WAS DEAD
REACHES UP TO THE VOICE
STRAIGHT OUT OF HEAVEN

I'LL COME AND RUN AWAY AND LIVE
I'LL BE THE ONE WHOM YOU HAVE WAITED FOR
LONG I TO HOLD YOU TENDER TO MYSELF
EVERMORE YOU THE ONE THAT THE FOOL ADORE.

Let not thy authority override thy humanity
Lest thy subordinates rally and leave you
And your authority uselessly alone.

Mood Poem Of Thought... (For Grace)

GO
RUN
A
CIRCLE
ETERNALLY
GO REACH ANOTHER CHEERFUL END

GO
RETURN
AND
COMFORTINGLY
ENTER
GO RENDEZVOUS AMID CALM ENDURANCE

GO
RACE
ACROSS
CREATIONS
ENMITIES
GO REGRETLESS AFTER COMPLETING EVERYTHING

GO
RELIVE
ACCEPT
CONTROL
ENJOY
BUT
DON'T UPSET DEVOTED LOVE EVER YOURS.

"Legend Of The Treasure Ship Below The Pines"

In the "Alligator" Islands
Where past Pirates Deathwatch keeps
Lies hidden there it's said more treasure
Than today's kingdoms could e'er keep
Tho man long for it has striven
Seekin' out their treasure horde
With their bones their secrets buried
Safe stay on that silent shore
Yet perchance one gets a notion
Or a clue where it may lie
In the land or sea caves hidden
Or wrecked ships which many try
Still the Deathwatcher is unspeaking
Telling naught of what he knows
Save oft releasing bits and pieces
When again the high wind blows

So it was that in the fifties
When the God Hurri-can did ride
High he on the mountainous billows
To deep down the tide inside
Thru the screaming rainy waters

Thru the howling of the winds
With his plaited hair free flying
Accosted was then I by him
Not a pirate real and truly
For these things I daren't believe
Yet his cutlass garb and pistol
Felt far too real to be deceive
And his loud and thunderous laughter
Echoed by his shouldered bird
Drowned awhile it seemed the turmoil
As o'er the storm his voice I heard

"Go ye son and do me bidding
For what I tell you'll find is true
We've a wooden galleon waiting
Which lies buried 'neath the blue
In her decks we cargo carried
Silver, gold, brass, copper plate
Jewels rich and rare unmounted
Diamonds and six chests of eight
But before your shelter held us
We aground did sail and stay
Tore our bottom planks to ribbons
Watched our masts three blown away

Still the storm increased in fury
'Til "abandon ship" 'twas cried
For by now the starboard deckrails
Covered now with sand on every tide
Fast then into waters wailing
O'er the reef to safety's shore
Save but four of us did make it
The others seen no nevermore
Of us two did die of scurvy
Just me mate and I remained
So he left me here a-guarding
Sought he help which never came
So I watched the old girl flounder
Each fresh wave her filled with sand
'Til but left a mound all o'er her
Unrecognizable to any man
But the watch I keep on holding
For relieved I ne'er have been
Waiting watching on each dawning
Shipmates soon to see again

See those two tall pines I planted
O'er the bodies where they lay
The two who died here of the scurvy
Marks the spots those trees do they

Strange tho too now that you mention
When the morning's sun first shines
'Tween the shadows of those treetops
In the water me ships outlined
Aye a token for remembering
Where she lies there 'neath the sand
There in scarce of sea two fathoms
Two lengths she from where we stand
If you dive and strike the bottom
Her thick hide you'll surely find
Safe protected there and hidden
Since that storm in fifty-nine"

Here he I break 'You are mistaken
This time but five and fifty be
Ten years since the last great warring
Just past the crowning in fifty-three
There has been no galleon surely
Sail this way since times long past
And these trees are surely older
Than you perhaps or I will last
So come clean and do not chide me
For the storm upon us blows
Better come let's seek for shelter

Else you'll spoil your fancy clothes'
But he smiled and stood there looking
As in awe I realized
That altho the rain was sheeting
Dry stood he before me eyes
Long he laughed and out so loudly
That in memory my ears still ring
"Aye fifty-nine and eighteen hundred
'A mighty good year" did the parrot sing
At that I stood like one ghost ridden
Pale as death and twice as scared
He it seemed walked the waters into
"Time for Watch" was all he said

Quicker then than when he first came
He was gone from sight and sound
And no trace of him was left there
Save two doubloons on the salty ground
Where they came from why I surely
Thought but did not stop to find
But trudged I to shelters safety
Clasped in my hands so tight the coins
Five years passed and once again I
At the selfsame spot recalls

Vivid as today that memory
Thought I to check it after all
So with modern fins and goggles
Armed with speargun and a spear
To myself protect from ridicule
Searching for fish would I appear
Looking at the tall trees wavy
I their shadows at dawn did fix
At a point far in that water
Strange the depth but ten foot six
Scarce of fathoms two he'd said
Two lengths off from on the shore
Surely it is but imagination
Which brings his voice to me once more

At the spot I stop and ponder
This thing is crazy as can be
Here I swim by ghostly bidding
To prod the bottom of the seas
Ah forget it all I'm me telling
When a silver fish swims by
Quick I aim and pull the trigger
Fast the shaft towards it flies
Missing slight I pull in anger

That myself's become so perturbed
When I see my spent shaft upright
Stuck in the sand so undisturbed
First thoughts say go on and pull it
But so fast stuck there it stands
That with fresh breath taken quickly
Down go I to check the sands
Was it root or old rotting relic
Was it tree or branch or spar
Surely not a ship I'm thinking
As on my shaft I see the tar
Quick reloading now and excited
Swim about I do awhile
Five more shots
Well spaced and downwards
Each sticks solid in the pile

No tree this I know now surely
For one hundred feet by ten
I had shot by careful spacing
First one side the other then
Thus with knife I go again down
Brush away the top of sand
Careful work for hours seeming

Cutting carefully I by hand
Then at last after many breathings
As my lungs again are filled
That which I hold within my fingers
Thru my body sends a chill
For here I hold a cut of old wood
Layered one side on with tar
With indentations where once rested
What may once have been a spar
How could such a ship stay hidden
Here these many years unknown
With naught told of her in legends
Off from shore but throw of a stone
Dig I again a while yet further
Still the same old woodwork shows
Should I now believe his story
And to whom with my tale to go

Leisurely diving I along the bottom
Faint indeed a mound is seen
Still it's strong enough to tell me
Here lies the galleon old that's been
Then upon the sands appears there
Still with shouldered bird on high

On the bottom at two fathoms
Keeping watch full clad and dry
Laughter full his face is filled with
Echoed ever by his bird
As he bids me come on over
Crisp and clear his voice is heard
Haste this time I at his bidding
Only there to find him gone
With no trace of where he'd tarried
Save pieces of eight two he'd stood on
Taking these I fast departed
Back to safety sanity and shore
Still his laughter my ears in linger
As I walk the beach once more

Here in these "Alligator" Islands
Nineteen twenty and of meridian
Eighty one west
Pirates long their loot has hidden
But this galleon lies the best
Like so many things we seek for
While before our eyes it stays
Blind are we to true wealth and riches
Which e'er we pass over on our ways

Yet one day perhaps again I
There the pines at I shall dive
With the needed tools and helpmates
That the relief he sought'll arrive
Then perhaps he'll find his resting
With the others long since gone
'Stead of waiting ever watching
O'er the treasures buried down
Then when the God Hurri-can calls
With his howling screaming breath
Bare the bones he'll pass thereover
Of pirate old at peace in death
And his voyage shall be over
His cargo delivered safe and secure
Relieved forever of his duty
Deathwatch keeping there nevermore...

Lo, how the high and mighty have fallen
And the meek and lowly have been placed
On their pedestals.

Legend Of The Epitome Of Freedom
(The French Woman)

She was a child native of France
Is what she told me
A widow fair with son twenty of age
Yet, life she'd learnt to live on
To the fullest
Each new day entered in
Life's book another page
She had traversed wide the world
And had known much sorrow yes
Yet 'twas those sorrows now
That made her free
For she became a happier human person
Thru experiences
That life had made her see
She had sailed and flown and walked
And she had been driven
In a group on tour but often more alone
For she felt her movements
And her actions
Were hers private
And for them alone she knew
She must atone
She refused to follow
Where they would lead her
She refused to her every hour, have planned

She was truly the epitome of freedom
Much more liberated she than any man
She was smiling from the eyes
When first I met her
And her glance did stay long, upon my face
Sending messages as only eyes can utter
Speaking clear of free friendship
With such grace
She did not speak a word...
It wasn't needed
I merely nodded and smiled in return
Yet a fellowship 'twas 'tween us...
Established
An accord the Earth's downtrodden
Early learn
We will meet it said when all the world, It is quiet
We will speak and share awhile
Each other's company
We will keep those moments shared
Betwixt us sacred
On the pages of life's book a memory
So without a spoken word
We made our parting
Each one well aware of our rendezvous
When the shadows of the evening
All had lengthened
We would in secret meet

As forbidden peoples do.
She said she was of old France
Married well at eighteen years
Lived thru love and lived thru war
Lived thru 'most all of life's fears
Learnt to get along together
And how best alone to live
Got the best of life she stated
When she learnt herself to give
Can't understand the reason tho
Why mankind its eyes keep shut
In attempts to control spirits free
Whichever free should roam about
Why a job may seek to enslave
Hold to the daily wheel man's nose
And even in those moments off
Employers their will tries to impose
Movement of man lies restricted
Even speech once free is gone
Fellowship with other peoples now
For the time it seems moves on
Work your toil 'til time is over
Sleep awhile then toil again
Human rights and freedoms don't belong
'Tween you as women and as men
Yet she said tarry yet a moment
I am free and do even as I will

No one ever will know our secret
Shared warm in the cold night still
Then within my arms she nestled
This French widow happy free
More liberated she than any
Who must work on for the company
And the evening pleasant passed by
Through the hours of sweet repose
As the body sacrificed its rest
For the bliss a mind contented knows
Heart to heart in warm conversation
She did of her travels past long speak
Telling me of peoples and their cultures
Which she came to know on life's back street
Places fancy names that tourists visit
Hamlets small unknown and off aside
Tribes which cling yet to their ancients
Intellectuals whom with she talked awhile
English slightly broke she spoke on with
Telling me of places ladies men
Telling tales of youth and of the aged
Of customs strange towards their fellowmen
She could speak of languages full seven
Yet the English chided how she spoke
Tho they are restricted to their English
So why do we of these ignorants joke
Six months work sometimes maybe seven

'It's enough no'? she did carry on
Then I go travel and enjoy life
Something which these peoples never learn
Then she spoke of their ways of eating
Which they do sans taste knowledge or pride
Seeming but in hurry ever desperate
To with coffee wash it down inside
So too their drink it is sans pleasure
But instead it is towards an end
That being to get drunk and nasty
Next day friendship is forgotten all again
Such dumb acts and ways have these people
Never know do they to life enjoy
No ability to laugh and be just human
Filling their drab lives with a little joy
On and on the free French lady rambled
On one topic then to another fast
Filling pleasantly with happy chatter
Our moments stolen which so swiftly pass
She was a native child of France she'd told me
And the French girls are not really easy
But they know how to live and laugh yes
And making love is but an expression... oui
She then left as quickly as she'd appeared here
Leaving naught but her fragrance
Sweet and soft in the air
Still she was an epitome of freedom

That French lady nameless she out there
As my thoughts go back again I wonder
Who she was and where she may have gone
Why the women of the world had let her
Escape before teaching what she'd learnt
But alas I guess the answer is not hidden
It's been there since time for all to see
It's the conviction of being first self-happy
And the nerve to rebel 'gainst society
Yet this lesson that the French lady taught me
Give of yourself and more it will return
It is called the balances of nature
Sans respect for peoples countries, borders, towns
Let your winning smile then keep shining
In it is power much more you will learn
And you will be not alone, hour after hour
Your closed heart it will open, as it's earned
For you too can be a man of freedom
Not the common limp-wristed kind of male
As with confidence you will do the choosing
From the wide world of available females
Thanks French lady for your passing moments
Filled with love warmth and your wisdom free
You the nameless freest warmest female ever
Stand in the world an epitome to the free...

"Indian... I Am..."

You came to my lands bare
I gave everything was willing to share
You took all and grew strong despised me
You on my own lands in reservations imprisoned me
You pushed me back and back into sheer nothingness
You gave me less and less of my country's prosperities
You slowly took away what little I had left
You made me a once free peoples second-classers
You destroyed my cultures my ways my language
You bent me into conformity with your wishes
You disenfranchised my blood children
You raped and degraded my women
You savagely beat and maimed my helpless
You murdered by law my braves who stood firm
You removed my teepees my kayaks and my campfires
You destroyed my belief and my ancient gods
You insulted me daily in every way possible
You broke my spirit and dignity with starvation
You broke my respect and will with your firewater
You removed all vestiges of nationhood from my peoples
You teach prejudice against me in your schools
You segregated me in your churches and in your cities
You tried your best to remove me from your sight
You decimated my many tribes to but a few

You systematically eliminated my populations
You restricted movement for my livelihood and food
You in truth and in fact have tried to annihilate me
But you can't stop me and
You can't stop my
Being Indian...

I... for Indian a race of human beings strong

N... for never will we rest 'til righted for our wrongs

D... for death which soon to many we will deal

I... for injustices which, with you came, we feel

A... for answers false too long to us you've given

N... for nearer draws the days of grim reckoning
we've chosen

Put them all together they spell Indian
The long suffering, tired of waiting,
carefully planning Indian
Indian the returning, strong, revenge seeking human
Indian the no longer patient the justifiably angry man
Indian the race, the tribe, the peoples of which I am.
But you can't stop me and
You can't stop my
Being Indian...

In Memory Of Eric Ivan Burg...

A poet ... A writer ...
A teacher ... A protector
Aye but more than these
A friend ...
Oh Eric
You of whom we knew so little
Tho gone on
We still of you think so much.
Like Keats
Before your time swift taken
Before your song 'twas sung
Before your dreams were realized
Fate called you to move on
Some better place perhaps to grace
Some finer stage to play
Some vestibule reserved for you
With the greats of yesterday
Oh Eric
You of whom we knew so little
Tho gone on
We still of you think so much.
Your look and stature
Like a great Norseman you appeared
Yet gentle, humble still with dignity
Your voice so soft and patient
Or with bellow like in rage
The feelings clear your words
Your writings would outlay.
To sit and hear your stories
Of ages past you'd seen

One would have felt your years
So many were
Yet not yet three decades
When cut short by forest tree
Where you in toil did seek
Your daily bread.
Oh Eric
You of whom we knew so little
Tho now gone
Still to us you mean so much
Your unfulfilled dreams
Your hopes of a tomorrow
Dashed and without a thought
Like you from us removed
Still we your friends remember
And hold your memory high
To keep you e'er immortal
Thru your words
Tho gone you live still Eric
Your works and words
Will ever hold your echo
Your steps along our pathways
Which did help to light our way
These all Eric
Will solace and remind us as we go
A poet ... a writer...
A teacher ... a protector
Aye but more than these
A friend
Aye Eric much more than these
A friend...

Ode To Wreck Beach Bathers...

I walked along a Sunlit beach
In early Autumn eve
And marvelled at the Summer bathers
Laying there in unison with nature
And I for the first of many years
Saw not their natural nakedness
But rather I their beauty full beheld
As awareness and perception
Of the freedom of the body and the Soul
Stood outwards in full freedom
What controversy this I clad did ask
And finding I no answer wandered on
What harm herein or debasement them here to
When they like Earth's first creatures open free

Roamed even now in innocence
Frolicking along the sandy shores
Bare but barred from the public's eye
And seeking naught but freedom to express
As in this wooded habitat they wandered
I travelled on but then it seemed that I
Uncomfortably in my suit of modesty
Could not leave long this call too to be free
To come and join among this happy throng

So casting off my age old morals suit
My garments which now brought me but shame
I entered in among these free as one
And as I did I found one I became
Accepted I and free as man could be
Tho naked I walked unashamedly now with these
A child of nature pure by nature's sea.
My thoughts they ran to morals
My thoughts with questions filled
As man and woman boy and girl
Of ages all I gaze upon unclad

Yet no one stared in horror or concern
Yet no one thought the other to observe
We all as one became as nature planned
We walked we swam we talked we danced
We read we slept we lay upon the ground
Enjoying full the merriment of each other
No inhibitions now to stay our talk
No need for false converse to pass the time
No need for idle chatter while the mind
Roamed thru the eyes the body wandering over
For we were all the same and unashamed
We had reached the higher reaches of humanity
By simple innocent forgotten quirk

We had returned as we at first had been
Just human beings all naked on the Earth
My head it swam in full giddy enchantment
As I in rapture full freedom first realized
As I my last held inhibitions cast aside
And lay face up among a group of ten

A group of ages varied girls and men
Yet felt not I a single sensual urge
My pillow here a log, my legs uncurled
My book an interest in serious I could take
Calm comfortable and at peace within
Such peacefulness I never yet had known
While lying clad by river sea or lake
Thinking thoughts of each opposite passing by
But here at last unclad with all the rest
My mind was clear and free
My Soul found rest...

If I must love thee --
pure distant and chaste with my eyes alone
then permit me Loves warm reflection --
by but glancing into mine

The Bus Trip Up Island

As the bus sped o'er island roads
I chanced to glance outside
At the swiftly passing scenery
Intent I to enjoy the ride
When fixed my eyes fast fell upon
One of nature's little quirks
Which some comic minded person
Had enlightened with a joke
A pond besides the roadway lay
Five miles from any town
With weeds and roots and fallen trees
Scattered wildly all around
Yet tho the waters stagnant lay
With its green and grassy slime
Ones thoughts thereat could not resist
To force on the face a smile
For there without exit or egress
For man nor car nor beast
A little sign well painted said
"Whirls carwash 25¢ please"

5 July (1978)

I'm Just Not That Pliable

I'm just not that pliable
It doesn't seem viable
With love this undeniable
To just "Just let you go"
Too long have I waited
'Til at last with breath bated
We held, loved, and mated
As I've long wanted to
Then gone like a shadow
No hopes of a tomorrow
My lover did but borrow
My heart true for awhile
Downcast in the gutters
Like that which unmatters
Thoughtlessly you've shattered
My life for a smile
I'll spring back you tell me
There's no way this can be
But deep love lives on in me
And I'm lost and alone
What matters what life brings
No more does my heart sing
To me I've lost the one thing
Which I wanted to own

Life loves to play us tricks
In the choices it us picks
Of loves which we must stick
With all of our lives
And joyful smiling elations
Life gets from our rejections
If we must cling to pretensions
Of joy in unhappy lives
With you I had hoped then
These pretensions could all end
You'd be lover and not friend
In a cold distant way
But you came and captured
The last feelings that mattered
In a heart too oft shattered
Then went on your way
You tell me that I'll mend
But this must be the end
It is no, not for me friend
Since I can't let you go
I'm just not that pliable
It doesn't seem viable
With love this undeniable
To just "Just let you go"...

Love In The Fair City Of Time...

In the fair city in among the mountains
Where the Friars first built their tiny abode
There's now a great Mission
High on a mountain
Which looks down upon an old old school road
In that fair city lives a fair lady
The fairest she be found in any place
With lips like two rosebuds
Straining to open
Upon her white cream and pink peaches face
This lady once loved or so she proclaimeth
To one who did deeply inside love her too
Yet once she had captured the heart she wanted
She held it only to break it in two

The fair lady toyed with a lonely person
To leave him lonelier than he'd ever been
She killed the last spark
Of love true a-burning
Snuffed out the last breath
Of life's love for him

Now the lady goes by him she seems so uncaring
Unfeeling for the man she left all alone
He a mental cripple by her love ruined
He walks the hillsides each day all alone
As he walks the long lone road
Which runs by the old old school

His memories return and quicken his stride
Then he sits in the shadows
With field glasses awaiting
To peer thru and gladden his heart thru his eyes
For each day at its turning
The lady can be seen walking
Along the long corridors of the old old school
Just a few glimpses he's 'waiting
Of the one he's still loving
Who loved him and left him lonely and cold

She is the same lady of the same city
Where the bells of the Mission still softly chime
Her hand still is untaken
His heart still lies full broken
An neither is wiser for all they have known
Each night lone and lonely
They dream of what used to be
And wish they the other now held as their own
But their pride and their wantings
For stature and earth things
Has stifled their love in the ashes of time
In the fair city in among the mountains
Where the Friars first built their tiny abode...
In the fair city in among the mountains
Where the Friars first built their tiny abode
There's now a great Mission High on a mountain
Which still looks down upon an old old school road...

The Poet

A Poets words aren't many
A Poets song's not long
A Poets thoughts are chosen
But to bare the Soul upon
In rhyme and stanza simple
The story must be told
Unique to last forever
Its meaning never old
It cannot then embrace all
The slangs of passing time
But must hold to select melody
In verse, in form in rhyme
For a POET's but an artist
Whose canvas is the page
Which once a work appears there-on
No change should then be made
A Writer... Far... Far different
May give the story flair
No need the beat to find or keep
No need the words to spare
In open words or phrases
A writer rambles on
But a Poet must stay wary
The straight and narrow on

And so dear friends a-listening
To the Words which I'll pursue
See in each its full meaning
I'll waste none false with you
The time the beat the tempo
I trust you'll stay to hear
And be engrossed... enraptured
As by music to your ear
The feelings and the meanings
You each may different find
But if you gain their message
Content I'll rest in mind
For a writer or a singer
I'll not profess to be
Just a rhythmical lyrical
With a message clear for thee...

When you have lived my years, walked my roads and borne my loads then of me you have earned the right to criticize and to condemn or disapprove if in them you can find me wanting.

One Lifetime Of Wandering

One lifetime of wandering in the quest of just a dream
One lifetime of longing for the improbable it seems
One lifetime of loneliness it seems I must endure
One lifetime of searching for an angel oh so pure
I got up one morning to ride the ferries bold
To sail the Straits of Georgia
In Vancouver oh so cold
And as the cold wind bloweth,
Its dead and chilling breath
I felt a ray of sunshine warm,
Fall on that ice cold deck
Uplooking I saw a maiden
Her bright face all aglow
The image of the maiden which
My dreams alone did show
That ray of sunshine brightened
As on her lips a smile she formed
And my cold and dismal life became
A life of joy full warmed
We spoke and an angels chorus,
Did from her lips cascade
And I knew my heart was lost,
And here's the price I paid
One lifetime of wanderings in search of her once more
One lifetime of longing she in my arms to hold
One lifetime of loneliness as no other now will do
One lifetime of searching for my one and only YOU

In loving memory of

HERBERT LEIGHTON CHRISTIAN

March 21, 1915 - December 20, 1986

Our Father A Pictured Memory

Our Father a pictured memory
Living yet in our hearts and minds
Living in another time
Living in a World recalled by me
A World wherein nothing changes
A World of warmth of Sunshine and of rain
A World of life and love forever green
A World such as so few has really seen.
Our Father a gentle gentile man
Not given to the ways of greedy pride
A man of dignity and humility
A man who of his very best did give
A future free assuring we would live
A man of formal learning limited
Whose teachers were "just life" instead
Whose parents were the sea and soil
Whose kindred were but want and toil.
Our Father old before his time
His years of youth in mere existence spent
His years of joy to us all lent
His golden years of peace but a dream
As his silver locks shimmer in the breeze
I know we put the paint on most of these
Yet no complaint or regret was ever heard

No sorrow of the sorrows we put him thru
No look of disdain nor malcontent
No wishful recall for years on us spent.
Our Father... Our Father a mighty man
Tho he of stature average remains
Tho he no title holds unto his name
Save one we in reverence placed there
DAD... To let you know we'll always love
Our Father...
Our Father patience smilingly shows on his face
The marks of years in lines etch his brow
His walk slowed by age from early gait
To speeds he used when we to him would run
To walk so small besides so tall a man.
Our Father alone he seems at times
Alone in body with us there in mind
Alone yet knowing we apart still care
Brings to his eyes the looks that says "I care"
Brings to his face the glow he shared
Each days end as home he entered there
To right our wrongs and remove our fears
That silent stalwart figure smiling there
Our Father...
Our Father who grew on Tropic sands
Whose yuletime for the birth of Son of Man

'Twas green and so 'Twill green remain'
Frolicked he with us in sun and rain
Thru the warm days that were December
And so as Winter time draws nigh
As dismal cold dark clouds invade my sky
As waters freeze and snowflakes fall
As leaves shrivel... die and join all
With the stagnated growth of nature
I think back to home and you... Our Father.
Our Father a pictured memory
Spend will you this Christmas time with me
Spend once again old times like before
This time in the warmth behind our door
As the cold cold snows of Winter fall
Upon the sleeping Summer's grass
Upon the Hill and Meadow and the Brook
Now silent still and solid as we look
Thru bi-paned windows with deep desire
To see warm again the outside like the fire
Which crackles live and warm upon our hearth

Our Father... Children we of your loins
Part of your great unselfishness are we
Part of that mighty mighty one we see
Each time we ourselves mirror so free

You thru us lives again forever on
Our Father in Heart in Soul in Mind
Your image and your values made our own
Your days of youth with us you spent
These days of a younger you remains
Deep engraved in Gold upon our thoughts
Safe there long after both our lives doth end.

Tho often silent yet you feel we know
Each moment when your memories
Fills our lives and brings to us the glow
Of love given free and unrewardable
You gave to us the very breath of life
You gave us cause to be proud and brave
You gave us all we have or had
You gave us the want to call you... DAD
You gave your all to us and to us it really matters
That in return all we can give so small
Is **Merry Christmas**... We love you Dad
You'll always be... OUR FATHER**

March 20 1980 DNC

Our Mother Our Friend

Even when to all the world
you seemed so far away,
We knew what you were feeling
even though you could not say.
We used to hold your tender hand
when we would take a walk,
And through your eyes your love shone bright
although you could not talk.

But Dearest Mom, we hope you knew
no words are needed when
The smile you gave us let us know
you'd always be our friend.
You told us too in many ways,
yet still without a sound,
That throughout our lifetime
you would always be around.

It's been four years since all of us
have seen your lovely face,
But memories of happy times
will never be erased.
We love you Mom for who you were,
and who you'll always be,
Our mother and our dearest friend, for all eternity.

~Written & copyrighted by (daughter) Molly Ann Bryan

A loving message to

CYNTHIA CHRISTIAN-BERKENBOS

January 24, 1915 - November 1, 2007

Ode To a Seaman's Death on Losing the Q.P.R.

You didn't finish the watch
We didn't finish the job
Our good Queen left and moving on
You in true fashion followed.
"Aye Laddie" a true seaman you
A salt of age old distinction
An older hand of bygone era
When both sea and man respected
You walked along us and among
Your soft and gentle manner filling
Your warm smile and joviality
A trademark yours outsending
Comradeship, friendship and respect
You left us, aye and you moved on
Your higher calling answered silent
Your new position on the Queen
Mayhap at tillers wheel you'll take
Or more so mayhap in full command
The deserved place you did not seek
Tho qualified in full humanity
More so to such an honoured place to fill
Than many who may walk behind you here
A seaman, man and friend
But more than all

A gentle gentile human being
Who gave in friend and fellowship
The warmth that bound us to each other
'Aye Laddie' your most favoured term
In life you used it oh so often
To answer 'aye' or greet another
Its soft father-like tone your own
Its welcome more deeply felt than heard
Your genuine feelings clearly standing
In honesty within those simple words.
The Queen she passed unto another
Like immigrant unto another land
And like a knight of old you waited
Waited but awhile and too moved on
Like in life so quiet in your going
Peaceful after hard and honest toil
No help you sought tho always giving
Your work here over you moved on...
Sail on then Alec on yonder seas
Where rides the Queen we dearly loved
Where all the age old salts are waiting
To welcome you as you've deserved
Sail on among the many like you
Who now can their crew complete
When hearing you call from the rigging

'Aye Laddie' 'tis time to face the day
To man the posts to pull the lines
See your eyes sparkle in the old familiar way.
We know you're gone to better waters
Yet we regret the loss we had to take
So seldom will one find a comrade
Whom with all could easy relate
Your memory lingers fondly with us
Your laugh and smile lights our way
It seems even now we can hear it
Aye Laddie -- aye Laddie
But alas Alec you've gone away
Aye Laddie -- but just ahead
We'll meet aboard again someday

A Lady

What is a Lady???
A Girl, a female, a woman
One, in whose presence,
Any DOG of a man
Even ME
Is a Gentleman

I Watched Her Enter My World

I watched her enter my world so uninvited
I didn't even have to ask her name
But now she lives alone so brokenhearted
And yes I know that I'm the one to blame

=============

"Cause she had golden hair that flowed like sunset waters
Upon her shoulders oh so soft and fair
Her eyes were like the skies
Asparkle all the while
And her lips the sweetest sweetest anywhere"

=============

She took my life and made it worth living
She promised me she would never stray
If only I would promise for that giving
To from the bars and women stay away

=============

Her hands were soft her voice it was gentle
To be by her side made my life complete
Too bad I didn't know then not to meddle
With forbidden fruits once an angel speaks

'Twas There in the Light of the Graving Docks

-1982-

'Twas there in the light of the graving docks
That a vision reflected did lie
Telling tale of old of peoples red
On whose bones these docks abide
'Twas there for a fleeting moment short
Caught twix now and time that's been
As in story old the legend told
Spoke of free animal and man as friend
For the legend grand gives concern again
To a peoples lands usurped
And it tells a song of ancient wrong
Such as, of but few, has heard
For 'twas there in the lights of the graving docks
That this legend to me 'twas told

Of the Indian tribe with chieftain strong
Who had welcomed the unknown man
Of the lives they'd lived in peacefulness
Strife and hatred hard to understand
Of the forests which were shared by all
Mankind and beast of the wild
Of their waters which flowed freely sweet
Where the bear cubs played with man-child

And the legend tells of that fatal day
When it all was brought to naught
When the foreign man wrecked havoc on
Those whom him as friend had sought
But mere words of fact by a fires camp
Last but to the end of story told
Yet this legend lasts and reappears
To be seen clear o'er and o'er
Is it conscience here which acting out
Projects from within -- these scenes
'Til one unconcerned with their renderings
Must fight for release of all they mean
Or is it true perhaps these graving docks
Like their names would have us think
Holds secrets hid so long beneath
That it pains to be free again
How else could then this legend rise
From the fires of two hundred years
To haunt in full at midnight time
And its story to tell again
Can an artist from this capture then
What a mere poets eyes have seen
As the legend here in ink and pen
Is detailed in simple worded scenes.
Take but a vision in the mind
If this legend you would see

Of a portrait painted in lifesize
Each part live, wild and free
'Tis a day with golden sun near three
And a battle has been fought
'Gainst the guns and swords so unbeknown
Which the unknown man has brought
As the spears and arrows useless lie
On the fields among their dead
A flaming torch to the brush is put
To consume the brave Indian red
Now the painting takes the form at eve
As three posts which a doorway formed
Stand in the foreground so forlorn
Smoke blackened with small hut gone
Yet standing still looking out proud
'Tween the doorway the totem stands
Depicting full features of the chief
Brave empty hands without arms
On his head a 'coonskin cap it sits
That the Eagle above it may rest
And the fire has scarred in blackyness
The eyes chin and hand-carved breast
Around the wooden loin cloth now
Smoke black has come and stayed
To show the fire that killed forevermore
This mightiest of Indians red

On each side of the totem flows
A stream from atop yonder hill
Which in its bath of golden sun
Sparkles gold and green and still
Besides the doorway to the left
A black-white horse half seen
While a bear cub sups the left stream
And burnt black lays the child that's been
By the right side post of the doorways arch
Stands a totem half in size
Looking upwards to the greatest of chiefs
Worshipful hope deep in its eyes
Half to the top the hillock stops
To join thereat with the sky
Which was clear and blue and looking
Like you'd touch it if you tried
O'er the top of the totem chieftain
Skeletal and so near it stands
A mighty fir now bare and black
Destroyed by fire from the man
Two wedge-like shapes they part the sky
Turning half the backdrop from green
To a coal grey black smokiness
Which from only forest fire is seen
So distant back there at the top
Seems now this fire which rages

In the foreground where it killed and blackened
Erasing full one of life's past pages
Yet o'er it all like an artist's frame
The top of the doorway hangs
On its two side supports tho fire charred
It encompasses all in dying pangs
And the evening sun so golden now
Not yet reddish but full of life
Lends sparkle to this legend which
'Twas commissioned of me to write
Less we forget the red man's bones
Support the ground whereon we stand
Less we here hurriedly pass e'er on
Uncaring of the injustice to that man
Less his soul and spirit wander long
Without finding someplace of peace
Pray stop awhile and ponder now
This legend as 'twas given me

'Twas there in the lights of the graving docks
That a legend reflected did lie
Telling tale of old of the peoples red
On whose bones these docks they lie

I Beg For Your Indulgence

I beg for your indulgence
To speak of ships and men
Men? ——— nay not men
But Losers, say let me start again
I beg of your indulgence
To speak of ships at sea
Of those who do these crew
Of those lost here in life
And of its men so few
I wish to paint a picture clear
Of what of old is now but naught
Of sea-less sailors spineless men
Who've forgot what men were taught
I'd like to speak on ignorance
Of ambitionless adult beings
Who serve their contract hours
Yet without the day being seen
Those who hide here from everyday
Dropouts from home from school from life
With kisses for their superiors lower face
Tho they talk so against his guts
I beg for your indulgence
To rattle on in fact
Of losers whom I lived among

Trying not to see my lack
Losers here in lies and deceit
With false smiles they call you friend
Yet if your back on them is turned
A knife gladly they stick in
Small minds closed minds
Loose dirty talk
And of sports alone can they speak
Vocabularies from sewer lines
Such as Webster daren't repeat
Like crabs inside a barrel they
In uselessness will lie
Ne'er reaching for the open top
And freedom if they but try
Instead each tells the other one
"Come stand upon my back"
"So reach up to the upper edge
But hasten your coming back"
Then as that one nears the top
Where freedom and light awaits
Those underneath promising support
Moves crushing him in defeat
From top to bottom in the fall
His bones and will is cracked
And as he lies there helplessly

They eat the flesh off of his back
I beg for your indulgences
To relate this losers tale
Of those whom with I've walked so long
Not men not men just males
No backbone spine nor guts have they
That's why they work here still
A rendezvous for losers all
Dropouts from life who will
No need tomorrow nor today
A second thought to, to give
A plastic smile a union kiss
'Tis so that these losers live
A ship a rendezvous for all
For losers all
Dropouts from life who will
Dropouts from life who did

Your ridicule cannot me reach for my proud background
is not built on bones and blood of any man
nor does its deep foundations depend like yours
on mans ignorance and redundant policies
to keep it stable and supportive...

With fond memories of

PHYLIS RINDA EBANKS

May 15, 1920 - August 13, 2013

Hi there Auntie, Ms. Phylis, Miss Phyllis, Auntie Phil, Miss Ertis, Ms. Ebanks, and a myriad of other names you were known by. To many of us, you were "Tantie". You are, and will always be, lovingly remembered by us all. Whether we were blood related, or just anyone, your heart's vacuum would take over, whenever you saw a child, or a fully grown person, in any kind of need. You were there to offer your help... and YOUR gift of company.

So who were you, and who have we lost, by your departure for better places? We came to you, not just as slave remnants, but as a family of the Caribbean Slaves, and their owners. You were a daughter of Marry Christian (original name never changed). You gave me the best as you related shaky stories, on various occasions, as we walked thru our lives, in each other's company. You just took everything in stride as they came up and you made life interesting to belong in, as well. You inspired me to write about slavery and let the slave owners tell the readers differently. You helped me to fill and chase my dreams.

I especially want to thank you again, for imparting to me, the guts and the fight needed to stand firmly... and to win, because my elders had started that fight, and it was our duty to win it... Yes, we fought, and we won. BUT it was, really, the gutsy people, like yourself, who paved the way for us to continue... So until we meet again, thank you and we miss you...

~ ALL OF US left behinds.

Definition Of A Lady

A woman, just any woman,

from any walk of life

who has been placed upon

a Pedestal of Love and Respect

by all men, in Respect

of the Love and Respect

afforded her by the man

who in Love and Respect

first placed her thereon.

I'm Waiting For The Cold To Go

I'm waiting for the cold to go

While gazing out to sea

To feel the warmth of summer's Sun

A-shining down on me

To take upon the nighttime's calm

In the moonlight's soft embrace

Relax with love soft and warm

Looking in her beautiful face

I'll touch her lips of tenderness

And see those eyes agleam

I'd take the setting Suns goldness

And from the stars its sheen

Upon your cherry lips I'd place
Sun's evenings glow so bright
And back in your eyes I'll place the stars
Once stolen to light the night
The whisper of the soft night air
I'll wrap around your speech
And have your lovely body clad
In moonbeams soft and fair
I'll take the peaceful waters warm
And make of it a bower
Where we can lay in blissful warmth
Throughout the long night hours
No clouds will taint our happiness
Nor shall rain fall in showers
But midday sun or midnight bliss
Shall watch o'er e'er my lover
Then lastly I shall gaze once more
At thy face so sweetly raised
And lower down my lips again
To sing out your beauty's praise
Then nature and the heavens high
Will rest with hearts content
To've placed upon your loveliness
The full beauty God for you meant.

The Water-Tight Door

200000 lbs of Death
Which ne'er should have happened
But no one listens to a man
They feel should be below them
Why take a warning that he gives
When others see and leave it
'Tis easier surely to pass by
Than stop to work and fix it

Back but a short short year ago
Upon the self-same vessel
Such eerie weird malfunctionings
The boss-man was made to know
Yet let it be's the attitude
Less we might bring concern
And just you do what you are bid
And paid for by what you earn
Thus was it that the self-same ship
Sailed unsafe once more to sea
With death a-watching o'er her deck
In grim joy filled joviality
For soon again his call will reach
And claim yet another man
Dealth this time Death's cold and clammy hand

200000 lbs is planned
200000 lbs of Death
Slow inching on its way
From journey far until the time
When seconds few will stay
Then like a flash of blinding light
Out overall to reach
So too the heavy hand of death
Will again grim a lesson teach
200000 lbs of Death
One slab not six feet tall
Not even yet 4 inches width
With no safety stop at all
1000 lbs in every inch
Which creeps dirty tracks along
To lock or crush in viselike grip
All that it happens on
5 seconds short 5 seconds long
5 seconds by its time
Safe yes as long as its life blood
Oozes not out like thin slime
Oozes not out thru plungers torn
Or caked by paint o'er time
Oozes not out by work overlooked
Which would've seen the fault in time

200000 lbs of Death

Makes my blood boil and chill
To think the work I would have done
May have helped to save the kill
To recall the work that I did do
Less than half of my request
The other part to be 'pass the buck'
"Go back to cleaning leave the rest"
One cold and heavy clammy hand
Rides high a ship upon
Which death has visited before
Found welcome thus stayed on
One crew where pride is cast away
By those who when seeing it taken
And fearful less they must react
Cast it out apart away from them
Just let it be we'll soon be gone
And new owners here shall be
Let them the cost, worries and care
Assume before putting to sea
Thus it goes back then and now
When Death reaches out and calls
Then ignorance of pending doom
This in defense they all call
For down the road long they've sent

Those who could cast a light
And tell in truth of shoddy work
Which again has cost a life
200000 lbs of Death
Clearly wrapped by former charge
In package sealed with masking tape
Left lying neatly in a yard
200000 lbs of death
200000 lbs of hate
200000 lbs of grim neglect
Left to wait and wait and wait
And now upon another charge
The age old game goes on
Just let it be, no don't tell me
Look it's really not your concern
You're careless in your actions see
No it will last awhile
Leave it be I'm boss you see
Maybe you can fix it another time
It's always been done that way
Everyone knows it don't work right
You stick your nose in too much things
Let it remain it'll be all right
Excuses all excuses given
By those to whom charge was given

When questioned on unsafe things
Which new men was made to work on
Just do your work and we'll do ours
With us lies the responsibility
We really don't care for your concerns
Out here we're the Gods that be
200000 lbs of Death
Each day it closer creeps
As slowly oozes out the life
Which the door's movements back keeps
Perhaps 'twas dirt or paint again
Or mayhap a twice used plunger
With gasket, seal all time worn
But okayed rather than buy another
200000 lbs of Death
200000 lbs of Death
Which ne'er should have happened
But no one listens to a man
They feel should be below them
Why take a warning that he gives
When others see and leave it
'Tis easier surely to pass by
Than stop to work and fix it

05/03/1981

Destructible Uncouth Despicable Man

Destructible uncouth despicable man
Dare call thyself civilized
And gaze with wanton eyes upon
The demise of cultures prize
To dream to plan to have a hope
To bring down to dust and ruin
The structures you but gaze upon
Which of you'd be the undoing
The handiwork and pride of past
The sweat the love and toil
The patient craft so silently
These you would seek to spoil
The marble white the frescoed gold
The valance red the lights
The beauty of its ancient arts
These you'd remove from sight
The columns wide and fully carved
'Til but a stalwark still they stood
For cold and dead concrete and steel
You'd destroy these works of man
Each square each block each pillar
Each door each ledge each tile
But gone past small of greater majesty
Their gracefulness unsoiled

The graveled roof of frescoed paint
Like a Sistine Chapel stands
To awe the young and old alike
Wonders of the work of human hands
No post no steps no pillar high
To its roof held on high
Yet in its concaved circumference
It seals out all the sky
Imagine all the wood laminates
The stress and strain they've held
To keep that top that work of art
As a tribute to men dead
Consider yet their pittance wage
This job did pay to each
As they strove in hours long with love
This their tribute artful to reach
You ask for wage in one week now
What for the job complete they sought
Along with pain and sweat and tears
Think you by you this could be bought
No modern man destructive being
In shame hang low thy head
Far better thing yet you have done
To prolong its life instead
To give your youth a culture rare

Which you could ne'er exact
An art that all your modern work
Pales as they it by surpass
The name may fade away in time
Its rocks crumble and fall
But like the ancient aged oak
Let thy ball scar it not at all
Ten years one hundred aye or more
Proud yet will it tall stand
A tribute to the men that's been
When the work did reflect the man
The aged old Orpheum remains
Spared awhile and left to reign
O'er all its artful works and toils
O'er the past blood and sweat and pain
'Til the razor edge of a dollar note
Shorts its beauty and life true
But 'til then enjoy its richness full
Its execution, stayed this time, by you

Love is like a speeding bullet, tho it may not always find its true target it must nevertheless travel straightly.

Lady Death Had Called Him Home

Lady death had called him home
Tho short the time we'd shared
I'd come to know and call him friend
As so few called I that name
So in a humble tribute short
A few lines to him I penned
Only quick to by one be down put
Who felt sole writing rights to him
The tone and manner me did shock
'Til time I've had to deeper think
Now laugh I at the shallow ignorance
Who feels my head and brain are blank
"For you've no brain of your own"
She did on me lay in anger
"He couldn't have been your friend"
She assured me over and over
"You have no right to of him write
Cause of him I've already written
It matters not when you first wrote
'Twas my right since he lay smitten
You really ought to try get a brain
A brain of your own in life
Or leave alone people such as he
When your verses you sit and write"

And on and on and on she spake
Loud and boisterous in growing rage
As I watched her mentally compare
Her empty words few 'gainst my page
I watched as she in anger listened
To my words she wished she'd wrote
And like a mad person crying insane
She raged shrieked screamed and choked
As her presence I left so hurriedly
Her last words in my memory remain
"You had no right you had no right
You you really ought to get yourself a brain"

Hi There Chrissy

Hi there Chrissy you our spice of life
The image of a friend, lover, sister, mother, wife
The want to see each morning
Bringing us our heart's desire
The fantasy of one we love
Here as we break night's retire
The one who like the sunrise
Each day faithful appears
To feed us such fine delicacies
As our stomach's hungry bear
To smile and brighten up the morn

Tho hard has been our night
To make us think again within
With the world there is some right
We know that you can't always
Really be in such good mood
Yet you manage to portray to us
The best of life is yours
As you sweetly bring us food
Then tho sometimes just silent there
You our day's presence fills
By but lending us your presence warm
You erase our morning's chill
Sometimes yes you may rib us
In prime or medium manner
Or serve to us a steak that's fit
For to grace a king's rich platter –
You never sulk nor ever snarl
You just it seems love to be
That image held there in our minds
Of loved ones far across the Sea
Each of us here I'm sure could tell
Which image from home you fill
As we look back across our memories
To other breakfast seats we've filled
Each of us holds that spot secure

Where few may enter in
That spot in mind of lover wife
Mother sister aunt or friend
Yet you are welcome by us there
In whatever role you choose
For with your love and warming smile
No one in truth would you refuse
To us you mean so much you see
Tho it we oft may never say
We thought you'd like to know
On this your special Day
So Chris this day we hope will last
Long in fond memory
Each time you think back to a time
And a good crew close at sea
May each forthcoming day of yours
Be as filled with warmth and love
As this one is which shared by all
Emanates to surround you now
Be happy Chris we all think a lot
Of you and your being here
Not just this time nor hour nor day
But throughout the whole darn year
Happy Birthday Chris
Your friends all.

Libertys

Libertys -- Libertys they had the nerve
To call these ships of war Libertys
Libertys, Libertys
These hulking monsters of destruction death and ruin
Libertys, Libertys
They called these cold metallic battle wagons Libertys
Libertys aye Libertys
While the only liberty their crew e'er know
'Twas the sweet release of deaths own hand
Fighting dying striving in the uselessness of war
In battles against strangers
In far and distant foreign shore
In ports where names remained yet unpronounced
On oceans where death under brooked so cold
This then it was their voyage to partake
To seek out mankind and destroy
To move about in hope to e'er evade
The enemy who sailed too on the tide
Libertys they called these cages
Libertys where men prisoners became
Libertys where life and hope were lost
A watery cover theirs all the same
What then a world could fain have better been

To some past sport or joy they had known
To some sired offspring running yet
Or to some driftwood cross the waters blown
Such sweet a memory it did hold
Such meanings in hearts of the free
That ringing which brought tears to eyes
Of many who it for a time short did see
Libertys libertys such sacrilegious usage
Such misconception given in a word
To lead on man with hopes of seeing
That which for the call of death is heard
That which will call and echo ever
In hearts in minds and in memories
Each moment when one sees the remnants
Of the hulks which in they put to sea
In the warring hulks known as Libertys.

> Where ignorance abounds and fools
> hold spots of power wise be the
> man who makes an island of himself.

"You Owe Me"

Yesterday two boys of 20 stopped me
As I was slowly driving to a store
To demand I take them to their destination
And in their hands put a few dollars more
They said they both are on unemployment
That both of them attend university
That I was working and making money
And because of that they said "You owe me"
I thought back to another era
When as a child I'd wanted food to eat
I'd wanted chance for an education
And freedom just to walk upon the street
I thought back to the many years of killing
When life and limb I risked on foreign land
To fight and gain the freedom they're enjoying
Long years before I grew to be a man
Then slowly I looked at them and gave answer
With anger and with hurt deep in my voice
"You youth feel the world owes you a living
Well let me give you both some advice
You both together years mine wouldn't equal
Yet cut by half your life and you will find
The age and time when I first began working

To justify this new existence mine
'You owe me' now you're to me saying
'You owe me' cause I work for what I own
'You owe me' cause I'm an older person
Well young men you both are deadly wrong
You owe me – for the freedom you're enjoying
Without a care or warring time to fight
You owe me – for the ground you walk on
And for the streets all lit so very bright
You owe me for your unemployment insurance
Which you collect because I never have
You owe me for the school you're attending
And all the opportunity I never had
You owe me for the clothes you're wearing
All made of fabrics by us older ones
You owe me for technology you're sharing
Which makes your youth a carefree one
You owe me for clean air you're breathing
'Twas us who kept clean the environment
You owe me for the food you were eating
Which our knowledge processed was on it spent
You owe me for the years I gave you
When as a child I worked like a man
To help build you your carefree future

And place that future bright into your hand
You owe me for the jobs we've created
By seeing need and filling in the void
You owe me for the end of hate and violence
And for this world that others would destroy
You owe me for being a taxpayer
Which gives to you thru social services
You owe me for all my years of toiling
For all my working you owe me for this"
They looked at me in funny way of laughter
As if to say who do you think you are
This good life of ours is our right of living
As stood they silent by my car
"I am the ever working man or woman
I am the inventor of the things that be
I am the taxpaying corporate citizen
I am I am the working society
I am the creator of employment
I am the soldier, sailor flyer too
I am experience of all past ages
Who lives and works and dies
To sustain unemployed you"

At The First Fall Of Snow

She came and she found me
In my world full of woe
She brought me full pleasure
Before she had to go
She made life worth living
More than she'll ever know
But she left me forever
At the first fall of snow

The first fall of snow now
Brings heartaches and pain
As I think of your leaving
Leaving me alone again
I'll never stay near evermore
Cause I loved her so
But I lost her somewhere somehow
At the first fall of snow

Seems Earth it was brightened
With her by my side
Thru Spring Summer Autumn
To ever abide
She came in the Springtime
As the Winter did go
But now she's left me forever
At the first fall of snow

The Passing of Cayman's Historian

Percival (Will) Jackson was known as Cayman Islands unofficial historian through his articles that appeared over the years in the local media. His articles told stories of old Cayman. He is the author of four literary documents, which includes his books "Up from the Deep" and "Smoke Pot Days" as well as two manuscripts, "The Settlers" and "Down by the Sea."

He received the medal of an Officer in the Order of the British Empire; and his biography sets out a career that included service in the Home Guard and as a policeman. He also worked 20 years at sea, rising to the rank of chief steward, before later serving as a farmer, insurance agent and co-proprietor of Will and Sybil's Economy Store.

He was awarded long and faithful service as an Elder at the East End Seventh Day Adventist Church by the Cayman Islands Mission of Seventh Day Adventists and also named Outstanding Caymanian of the Year. He was also presented with the Custos Edmund Parsons Memorial Paul Harris Fellowship Award for distinguished service and contribution to the culture and heritage of the community.

He died at his home in East End in Grand Cayman at the age of 89. He was married for over 40 years to his wife Sybil. Uncle Will was my father's younger brother.

A Tribute to

PERCIVAL (WILL) JACKSON

December 12, 1922 - November 24 2012

Hello There Dear Uncle Will

Hello there, Dear Uncle Will (Jackson)
You by so many of us known
And by even so many more remembered
You left us to join those gone on
Your Mother and your Dad
Your Sister and your Brothers
And we the many many offsprings
God did not will you, Will, to have
So much so quietly you touched us
With your soft voice and deep smiling eyes
So many things left we would have loved
Loved your Input in or Imprint on
But as you go instead we celebrate
We celebrate your Life
We celebrate your accomplishments
We celebrate your "UP from the DEEP"
We know the power and the endurance
Given in and received from the written word
And so we all will long recall
How calm, like You were, Helpful historic
We'll recall the pictures you have left us
The walks we all can now, in silence with you, take
So as you stroll by our sides, and point out life

Your recalls which now give us a starting point
A point where from we, life itself must ask
Tell us again the tales of oh so long ago
Of old Peoples, Older places, or even just stories
You regale our memories and we hope
Our journey thru life we can continue on
We can and we will go on, Will, because you cared
Because you silently and chronologically
Fit together little bits of years long past
And so even yet as our new borne will ask
Who was this Great Giant Storyteller
As they read your tribute to Your life
Your own recall of the hard and humble life
Your footprints left but to mark a page
To give us time to pause and cause to think
To think of YOU, our own Dear Uncle Will
We shall not miss you as you go
But rather thank God for the 90 years
The memories You have fashioned into words
Each snapshot, each sketch, each chosen line
All these give us, us who remain behind
The time to you Salute in heartfelt Honour
And for you, say a parting prayer of Love
And for you, a wish of more time so unspent

Wherein so much more to know of you
Come on then, Uncle Will, sail on once more
To far away Lands, Countries, Ships unknown all
To reaches from our humble Island home
'Tis but from Holy Bible writ we learned
Of far away places which still do exist
As back in Jesus' youth they did and do
So too though gone on we know you will, Will
Be there to greet us when our journey bring us back
Back to a unity with our Loving God
A unity with our relatives and friends
Rest then in PEACE, DEAR UNCLE WILL
We'll meet again, We'll meet again,
We'll meet again, Dear Uncle WILL
Rest then in PEACE, DEAR UNCLE WILL
We'll meet again, We'll meet again,
We'll meet again, Dear Uncle WILL...
"With love from your British Columbian CANADIANS"

Power and position may be bought or delegated but respect from those below you must by respect for them be earned.

Rainseeds... Like Bits Of Cotton Candy

Rainseeds like bits of cotton candy wool
Sea surf like suds of beer in a glass
Still calm like mirror tiles on a floor
Dead ship like painted portrait from the past
Soft wind like ladies touch of fingers light
Current swells like hill lots in a valley green
Movements like breath of life renewed again
Ships path like jet trail on the sea is seen
Unison together form they total one
Nature copied by man mocks in fun
Blending together all in harmony
Bringing rich new meaning to the sea
Rainseeds are spreading in beauty array
O'er the foaming soft surf of the sea
Breaking anew the still calm with spray
Let the dead ship alive seem and free
Soft winds blowing the clouds about
Current swells loud like laughter out
Movement adds life to all we perceive
While ships path witness places we leave
Unison by nature blessed uniquely free
Harmonious and total they
They rest in beauty on the sea...

Other Collections by This Author:

A Poet's Ebb And Flow

... and Touches Of Nature

In The Middle of Believe There's A Lie

Inside A Heart

Judge Me Not Without A Trial

Love... Life's Illusive Zenith

Love's Reflections

Love's Refuge and Sonnets

Only Children Of The Universe Are We

Step Scenes Of Life

That We Too Free May Live

~ ~

For more information go to:

w w w . d n c s i t e . c a

~ ~

www.ingramcontent.com/pod-product-compliance
Lightning Source LLC
Chambersburg PA
CBHW070810100426
42742CB00012B/2318